OVERCOMI NG BREAKUP GRIEF

Establishing Healthy Limits for Emotional Healing and Growth

George S. Scott

George S. Scott

TABLE OF CONTENTS

INTRODUCTION

Breaking up is never easy. It's a painful experience that can leave us feeling lost, alone, and overwhelmed with grief. In this book, I invite you to join me on a journey of overcoming breakup grief, where we'll navigate the turbulent waters of heartache and emerge stronger, wiser, and more resilient.

My journey into overcoming breakup grief began with a shattered heart and a sense of despair that seemed insurmountable. I remember the day when I received that crushing phone call, the words piercing through my chest like a dagger. I was left reeling, wondering how I would ever pick up the pieces of my shattered dreams.

But amidst the pain and despair, I found a glimmer of hope. It was during those darkest moments that I discovered the power of resilience and the strength of the human spirit. As I began to navigate the ups and downs of grief, I unearthed a newfound sense of self-awareness and inner strength that I never knew existed.

Through the tears and the heartache, I embarked on a journey of self-discovery and healing. I delved deep into my emotions, confronting the pain head-on and allowing myself to feel, to heal, and to grow. And with each passing day, I found myself emerging from the shadows of grief, stronger and more resilient than ever before.

Now, I share my journey with you in the hopes that it may offer solace, guidance, and inspiration to those who are navigating their path through breakup grief. Together, we'll explore practical strategies for coping with heartache, rediscovering joy, and reclaiming our sense of self-worth.

So, if you're ready to embark on a journey of healing and transformation, I invite you to dive into the pages of this book with an open heart and an open mind. Let's navigate the twists and turns of breakup grief together, and emerge on the other side as stronger, wiser, and more resilient individuals. It's not easy, but the reward is immense. Let's begin.

CHAPTER ONE: COPING WITH THE INITIAL SHOCK

Breakups can often leave us feeling as though the ground beneath our feet has suddenly vanished, plunging us into a state of shock and disbelief. In this chapter, we'll explore how to recognize the signs of shock and disbelief, strategies for managing overwhelming emotions and finding support during the early stages of a breakup.

Recognizing the Signs of Shock and Disbelief

When a relationship comes to an end, it's common to experience a sense of disbelief and numbness. You may find yourself questioning whether the breakup is real or feeling as though you're living in a fog. Recognizing the signs of shock and disbelief is the first step toward coping with these overwhelming emotions.

Signs of shock and disbelief may include:

Feeling numb or emotionally detached
Denying the reality of the breakup
Experiencing physical symptoms such as rapid heartbeat or shallow breathing
Difficulty concentrating or making decisions
A sense of disorientation or feeling disconnected from reality.

Real Life Experience:

When Sarah's partner of five years abruptly ended their relationship, she found herself in a state of shock. "I couldn't believe it was happening," she recalls. "I kept replaying our last conversation in my mind, hoping it was just a bad dream."

Strategies for Managing Overwhelming Emotions

While experiencing shock and disbelief is a natural response to a breakup, it's important to find healthy ways to cope with these overwhelming emotions. To help you deal with this difficult time, we've put together some strategies:

Allow Yourself to Feel: It's okay to feel a wide range of emotions, including sadness, anger, and confusion. Permit yourself to experience these emotions without judgment or criticism.

Practice Self-Care: Take care of your physical and emotional well-being by engaging in self-care activities that nourish your mind, body, and soul. This may include getting enough sleep, eating nutritious meals, exercising, and spending time with loved ones.

Express Yourself: Find healthy outlets for expressing your emotions, whether it's through journaling, talking to a trusted friend or family member, or engaging in creative activities such as art or music.

Set Boundaries: If interacting with your ex-partner is causing you additional distress, it's okay to set boundaries to protect your emotional well-being.

This may involve limiting contact or taking a break from communication altogether.

Seek Professional Help: If you're struggling to cope with overwhelming emotions or find yourself unable to function in your daily life, consider seeking support from a therapist or counselor who can provide guidance and support.

Real Life Experience:

John found solace in journaling as a way to express his emotions during the initial shock of his breakup. "Writing down my thoughts and feelings helped me make sense of what was happening," he shares. "It was like a release valve for all the pent-up emotions I was experiencing."

Finding Support During the Early Stages

During the early stages of a breakup, it's important to lean on your support network for emotional support and encouragement. Surround yourself with friends, family members, and other loved ones who can offer empathy, understanding, and a listening ear.

Seeking support from others can help you feel less alone and more supported during this challenging time. Whether it's talking to a friend over coffee, joining a support group, or seeking guidance from a therapist, finding support can provide comfort and validation as you navigate the initial shock of a breakup.

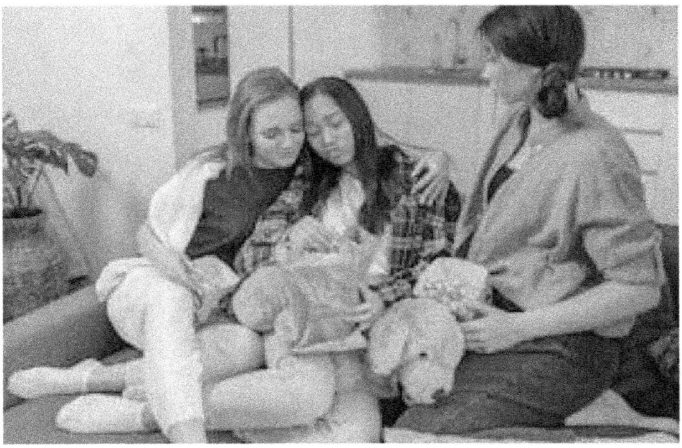

Real Life Experience:
After her breakup, Emma found comfort in spending time with her close friends and family members. "Having people I could lean on and talk to made all the difference," she says. "Their support helped me feel less alone and gave me the strength to keep moving forward."

In conclusion, coping with the initial shock of a breakup can be overwhelming, but it's important to remember that you're not alone. By recognizing the signs of shock and disbelief, finding healthy ways to manage your emotions, and seeking support from others, you can navigate this challenging time with resilience and strength. Remember to be gentle with yourself and take things one day at a time as you begin the healing process.

CHAPTER TWO:
NAVIGATING THE DEPTHS OF SADNESS

In the aftermath of a breakup, it's common to find yourself engulfed in waves of profound sadness and despair. In this chapter, we'll explore how to understand the depths of sadness and despair, process feelings of loss and longing, and discover coping mechanisms for dealing with profound sadness.

Understanding the Depths of Sadness and Despair

Sadness is a natural response to loss, and after a breakup, it's not uncommon to experience feelings of deep sorrow and despair. Understanding the depths of sadness involves acknowledging the intensity of your emotions and recognizing that it's okay to grieve the loss of the relationship.

When you're navigating the depths of sadness, it's important to:

Give Yourself Permission to Grieve: Allow yourself to feel the full spectrum of emotions that come with loss, including sadness, anger, and pain. Don't judge or criticize yourself for feeling sad—it's a necessary part of the healing process.

Validate Your Emotions: Remind yourself that it's normal to feel sad and that your feelings are valid. Avoid dismissing or minimizing your emotions, and instead, offer yourself compassion and understanding.

Seek Understanding: Take time to reflect on the root causes of your sadness. Are you mourning the loss of the relationship itself, or are you grieving the dreams and expectations you had for the future?

Understanding the source of your sadness can help you process your emotions more effectively.

Personal Experience:

After my breakup, I found myself consumed by a profound sense of sadness, unlike anything I had ever experienced. I felt as though I was drowning in a sea of tears, unable to find my way to the surface. Understanding the depths of my sadness required me to confront the pain head-on and acknowledge the reality of my loss.

Processing Feelings of Loss and Longing

Processing feelings of loss and longing is an essential part of healing from a breakup. It involves coming to terms with the reality of the relationship's end and finding healthy ways to cope with the absence of your ex-partner in your life.

Here are some strategies for processing feelings of loss and longing:

Allow Yourself to Grieve: Permit yourself to mourn the loss of the relationship and the future you had envisioned with your ex-partner. Cry, journal, or express your emotions in whatever way feels most cathartic for you.

Practice Acceptance: Acceptance doesn't mean that you have to like or approve of the breakup—it simply means acknowledging the reality of the situation and letting go of resistance. Embrace the mantra, "It is what it is," and focus on accepting things as they are, rather than dwelling on how you wish they could be.

Focus on Self-Compassion: Be gentle and kind with yourself as you navigate the grieving process. Practice self-care activities that nourish your mind, body, and soul, and prioritize your emotional well-being.
Personal Experience:

Processing the feelings of loss and longing after my breakup was one of the most challenging aspects of my healing journey. I found myself longing for the comfort and familiarity of my ex-partner's presence, even as I grappled with the reality of our separation. It took time, patience, and self-compassion to come to terms with the depth of my emotions and find a sense of peace within myself.

Coping Mechanisms for Dealing with Profound Sadness

Coping with profound sadness requires finding healthy ways to manage your emotions and nurture your well-being. While there's no one-size-fits-all solution, here are some coping mechanisms that may help:

Engage in Self-Care: Take care of your physical and emotional needs by engaging in activities that bring you comfort and joy. This may include exercise, meditation, spending time in nature, or indulging in hobbies that uplift your spirits.

Seek help: seek support and advice from friends, family members, or a counselor. Talking to someone you trust can provide validation, perspective, and a sense of connection during difficult times.

Practice Mindfulness: Stay present and grounded in the moment by practicing mindfulness meditation or deep breathing exercises. Mindfulness can help you cultivate awareness of your thoughts and emotions without judgment, allowing you to find peace amidst the storm of sadness.

Express Yourself Creatively: Channel your emotions into creative outlets such as writing, painting, or music. Expressing yourself creatively can be a powerful way to process your feelings and find solace in self-expression.

Personal Experience:

During the darkest days of my breakup, I found solace in practicing yoga and meditation. These practices helped me quiet my mind, soothe my soul, and reconnect with a sense of inner peace. By prioritizing self-care and seeking support from loved ones, I was able to navigate the depths of my sadness with courage and resilience.

If you want to navigate the depths of sadness after a breakup, you will encounter some challenging situations but it is a necessary part of the healing process. By understanding the nature of your emotions, processing feelings of loss and longing, and finding healthy coping mechanisms, you can gradually emerge from the darkness and embrace the light of healing and hope. Remember, it's okay to feel sad—it's a sign of your capacity to love deeply and to heal.

CHAPTER THREE: DEALING WITH ANGER AND RESENTMENT

Anger and resentment are common emotions experienced during breakup grief, and they can be powerful forces that complicate the healing process. In this chapter, we'll explore the role of anger and resentment in breakup grief, healthy ways to express and release anger, and the importance of forgiveness in letting go of resentment.

Exploring the Role of Anger and Resentment in Breakup Grief

Anger and resentment often arise as a response to feelings of betrayal, injustice, or hurt during a breakup. You may feel angry at your ex-partner for ending the relationship, resentful towards yourself for perceived mistakes, or even angry at the situation itself. Understanding the role of anger and resentment in breakup grief is crucial for processing these emotions effectively.

During my breakup, I found myself consumed by feelings of anger towards my ex-partner for the pain they had caused me. I also felt resentful towards myself for not seeing the signs earlier. Recognizing and acknowledging these emotions was the first step toward healing.

Healthy Ways to Express and Release Anger

While anger is a natural and valid emotion, it's essential to find healthy ways to express and release it without causing harm to yourself or others. Here are some strategies for constructively managing anger:

Physical Activity: Engage in physical activities such as exercise, sports, or even punching a pillow to release pent-up energy and frustration.

Journaling: Write down your thoughts and feelings in a journal to process and release anger in a safe and private space.

Deep Breathing: Practice deep breathing exercises to calm your mind and body when you feel overwhelmed by anger.

Talking it Out: Express your feelings of anger to a trusted friend, family member, or therapist who can offer support and validation.

Mindfulness Meditation: Practice mindfulness meditation to observe and accept your anger without judgment, allowing it to pass without reacting impulsively.

By incorporating these strategies into my own life, I was able to channel my anger into productive outlets such as journaling and physical exercise, which helped me release tension and regain a sense of inner peace.

Forgiveness and Letting Go of Resentment

Forgiveness is a powerful tool for releasing resentment and moving forward with your life after a breakup. It's not about condoning or excusing the actions of your ex-partner but rather freeing yourself from the burden of carrying anger and bitterness.

Forgiveness involves:

Acceptance: Accepting that what happened cannot be changed and releasing the desire for revenge or retribution.

Compassion: Cultivating compassion for yourself and your ex-partner, recognizing that everyone makes mistakes and deserves understanding.

Letting Go: Letting go of the past and releasing the emotional attachment to feelings of resentment, allowing yourself to move forward with a sense of peace and closure.

Forgiveness was a challenging but transformative process for me. It allowed me to release the weight of resentment that had been holding me back and embrace a future filled with hope and possibility.

In conclusion, dealing with anger and resentment is an essential aspect of the breakup grief process. By exploring the role of these emotions, finding healthy ways to express and release anger, and embracing forgiveness, you can navigate the challenges of breakup grief with grace and resilience. Remember, healing takes time, but by confronting your emotions head-on and practicing self-compassion, you can emerge from the darkness of anger and resentment into the light of forgiveness and healing.

CHAPTER FOUR: FINDING MEANING AND ACCEPTANCE

In the aftermath of a breakup, finding meaning and acceptance can be a transformative journey towards healing and growth. In this chapter, we'll explore how embracing acceptance, seeking meaning and growth from the breakup experience, and cultivating self-compassion and self-love can help you navigate the challenges of heartache and emerge stronger than before.

Embracing Acceptance as a Key Step in the Healing Process

Acceptance is the cornerstone of healing from a breakup. It involves acknowledging the reality of the situation, letting go of resistance to what cannot be changed, and embracing the present moment with openness and grace. While acceptance may not come easily, it is a crucial step towards finding peace and moving forward with your life.

During my breakup, I struggled to accept the end of the relationship and the pain it brought. However, as I began to embrace acceptance, I found a sense of liberation and empowerment. Acceptance allowed me to release the grip of resistance and surrender to the natural flow of life, opening the door to healing and transformation.

Seeking Meaning and Growth from the Breakup Experience

While breakup grief can feel overwhelmingly painful, it also presents an opportunity for profound growth and self-discovery. By seeking meaning and growth from the breakup experience, you can uncover valuable lessons, cultivate resilience, and emerge from the darkness with newfound wisdom and strength.

To find meaning and growth from your breakup experience, consider:

Reflecting on Lessons Learned: Take time to reflect on the lessons and insights gained from the relationship and its end. How can you apply these lessons to future relationships and personal growth?

Identifying Silver Linings: Look for silver linings amidst the pain and heartache. Perhaps the breakup freed you from a toxic relationship or opened doors to new opportunities and experiences. By focusing on the positive aspects of the breakup, you can shift your perspective and find hope in despair.

Setting Intentions for Growth: Intentionally cultivate personal growth and development in the wake of the breakup. Set goals for yourself, whether they involve pursuing new hobbies, investing in self-care, or deepening your connections with others. By committing to your growth journey, you can turn the pain of the breakup into a catalyst for positive change.

Cultivating Self-Compassion and Self-Love

Self-compassion and self-love are essential ingredients for healing from a breakup. They involve treating yourself with kindness, understanding, and acceptance, even in the face of pain and imperfection. By nurturing self-compassion and self-love, you can cultivate inner strength, resilience, and a deep sense of worthiness.

To cultivate self-compassion and self-love:

Practice Self-Care: Prioritize your physical, emotional, and mental well-being by engaging in self-care activities that nourish your body, mind, and soul.

Challenge Negative Self-Talk: Notice and challenge self-critical thoughts and beliefs that undermine your sense of worthiness and self-love. Replace negative self-talk with affirmations of kindness, compassion, and encouragement.

Forgive Yourself: Release yourself from the burden of self-blame and guilt by practicing forgiveness towards yourself. Recognize that you are human, imperfect, and deserving of love and compassion, regardless of past mistakes or shortcomings.

In this concluding part of this chapter, finding meaning and acceptance in the aftermath of a breakup is a transformative journey that requires courage, resilience, and self-compassion. By embracing acceptance, seeking meaning and growth from the breakup experience, and cultivating self-compassion and self-love, you can navigate the challenges of heartache with grace and emerge stronger and wiser than before. Remember, healing is a journey, not a destination, and by honoring your experiences and embracing your inherent worthiness, you can pave the way for a brighter and more fulfilling future.

CHAPTER FIVE:
REBUILDING SELF-IDENTITY AND CONFIDENCE

In this chapter, we'll explore the journey of rebuilding self-identity and confidence by rediscovering yourself, building self-esteem, and setting goals for personal growth.

Rediscovering Who You Are Outside of the Relationship

One of the first steps in rebuilding self-identity is to rediscover who you are outside of the relationship. When we're in a partnership, it's easy to become intertwined with our partner's identity, often losing sight of our wants, needs, and passions.

To rediscover yourself:

Reflect on Your Passions: Take time to reflect on the activities, hobbies, and interests that bring you joy and fulfillment. Reconnect with old hobbies or explore new ones that pique your interest.

Spend Time Alone: Embrace solitude as an opportunity to get to know yourself on a deeper level. Spend time alone doing activities that nourish your soul and allow you to connect with your innermost desires and values.

Explore Your Values: Reflect on your core values and beliefs, and consider how they align with your actions and choices. Clarifying your values can provide a solid foundation for building a strong sense of self-identity.

Building Self-Esteem and Confidence After a Breakup

A breakup can deal a blow to our self-esteem and confidence, leaving us feeling insecure and unworthy. However, rebuilding self-esteem is possible with time, effort, and self-compassion.

To build self-esteem and confidence:

Practice Self-Compassion: Be gentle and kind with yourself as you navigate the challenges of rebuilding self-esteem.

Celebrate Your Strengths: Identify and celebrate your strengths, talents, and accomplishments. Acknowledge the unique qualities that make you who you are and take pride in them.

Challenge Negative Self-Talk: Notice and challenge self-critical thoughts and beliefs that undermine your self-esteem. Replace negative self-talk with affirmations of confidence, worthiness, and self-love.

Setting Goals and Embracing New Opportunities for Personal Growth

Setting goals for personal growth is a powerful way to rebuild self-identity and confidence after a breakup. By embracing new opportunities and challenging yourself to grow, you can create a brighter and more fulfilling future for yourself.

To set goals and embrace new opportunities:

Identify Your Values and Priorities: Clarify your values, passions, and priorities, and use them as a guide for setting meaningful goals. Align your goals with your core values to ensure they resonate with your true self.

Break Goals into Manageable Steps: Break larger goals into smaller, manageable steps that you can take action on. Celebrate each milestone along the way, and don't be afraid to adjust your goals as needed based on your progress and priorities.

Embrace Growth Mindset: Adopt a growth mindset by viewing challenges as opportunities for learning and growth. Embrace the journey of self-discovery and personal development, and be open to embracing new opportunities that come your way.

Conclusion

In conclusion, rebuilding self-identity and confidence after a breakup is a journey of self-discovery, self-compassion, and personal growth. By rediscovering who you are outside of the relationship, building self-esteem and confidence, and setting goals for personal growth, you can emerge from the pain of heartache with renewed strength, resilience, and purpose. Remember, the breakup may have ended a chapter in your life, but it's also the beginning of a new chapter filled with endless possibilities for growth and fulfillment.

CHAPTER SIX: NURTURING HEALTHY RELATIONSHIPS

Building healthy relationships after a breakup is essential for your emotional well-being and personal growth. In this chapter, we'll explore the key elements of nurturing healthy relationships, including establishing boundaries and self-care, recognizing red flags and toxic patterns, and cultivating healthy communication and intimacy.

Establishing Boundaries and Self-Care in Future Relationships

Setting boundaries is crucial for maintaining healthy relationships and preserving your well-being. Boundaries define what is acceptable and unacceptable behavior in a relationship, ensuring that your needs and values are respected.

Here's how to establish boundaries and prioritize self-care in future relationships:

Identify Your Needs: Take time to reflect on your needs, values, and boundaries. What are your non-negotiables in a relationship? What actions do you hate? Clarifying your needs will help you establish clear boundaries with future partners.

Communicate Effectively: Communicate your boundaries openly and assertively with your partner. Be clear about your limits and expectations, and express them respectfully and compassionately. Know fully well that healthy relationships are established on mutual respect and understanding.

Prioritize Self-Care: Prioritize self-care and self-love in your relationships. Make time for activities that nourish your mind, body, and soul, and don't hesitate to prioritize your well-being.

Recognizing Red Flags and Toxic Patterns

To nurture healthy relationships, it's crucial to recognize red flags and toxic patterns early on. Red flags are warning signs that indicate potential issues or concerns in a relationship, while toxic patterns are harmful behaviors or dynamics that can erode trust and intimacy.

Here are some common red flags and toxic patterns to watch out for:

Lack of Respect: Disrespectful behavior, such as belittling, criticizing, or demeaning comments, is a major red flag in any relationship.

Control and Manipulation: Control and manipulation are toxic patterns that can manifest in various forms, including gaslighting, coercion, and emotional blackmail.

Lack of Communication: Poor communication or an unwillingness to address conflicts and issues openly and honestly can indicate underlying problems in a relationship.

Isolation: Attempts to isolate you from friends, family, or other sources of support are manipulative tactics often employed in toxic relationships.

Cultivating Healthy Communication and Intimacy

Healthy communication and intimacy are the foundation of strong and fulfilling relationships. Cultivating open, honest, and respectful communication, as well as fostering intimacy and connection, can strengthen the bond between you and your partner.

Here's how to cultivate healthy communication and intimacy in your relationships:

Practice Active Listening: Listen actively to your partner's thoughts, feelings, and concerns without judgment or interruption. Validate their experiences and show empathy and understanding.

Express Yourself Authentically: Communicate your thoughts, feelings, and needs openly and honestly with your partner. Be vulnerable and authentic in your communication, and encourage your partner to do the same.

Create Rituals of Connection: Foster intimacy and connection by creating rituals of connection, such as regular date nights, shared activities, or meaningful conversations. These rituals can strengthen your bond and deepen your emotional connection.

Seek Professional Help if Needed: If you're struggling to navigate communication or intimacy issues in your relationship, don't hesitate to seek professional help from a therapist or counselor. Therapy can provide valuable tools and strategies for improving communication and fostering intimacy.

Lastly, nurturing healthy relationships requires intentional effort, communication, and self-awareness. By establishing boundaries and prioritizing self-care, recognizing red flags and toxic patterns, and cultivating healthy communication and intimacy, you can create a relationship built on mutual respect, understanding, and love. Remember, healthy relationships take time and effort to nurture, but the rewards of a fulfilling and supportive partnership are well worth it in the end.

CHAPTER SEVEN:
HONORING THE PAST AND EMBRACING THE FUTURE

As you journey through the aftermath of a breakup, it's essential to find a balance between honoring the past and embracing the future. In this chapter, we'll explore the importance of reflecting on the positive memories of the past relationship, letting go of regrets, and creating a vision for the future filled with hope and possibility.

Reflecting on the Positive Memories of the Past Relationship

While the pain of a breakup may overshadow the positive memories, it's important to take time to reflect on the moments of joy, love, and connection you shared with your former partner. These memories are a testament to the depth of your emotional bond and the meaningful experiences you shared.

Take a moment to:

Acknowledge the Good Times: Recall moments of laughter, warmth, and affection shared with your ex-partner. These memories serve as a reminder of the love that once existed between you and can provide comfort during difficult times.

Express Gratitude: Express gratitude for the lessons learned and the growth experienced during the relationship. Every relationship, whether it ends in heartache or not, offers valuable opportunities for personal development and self-discovery.

Celebrate Your Growth: Reflect on how you've grown and evolved as a person as a result of the relationship. Recognize the strengths and qualities you've developed and carry them forward into your future endeavors.

Let go of regrets and embrace new beginnings

Regrets and "what ifs" are common after a breakup, but dwelling on them can hinder your ability to move forward and embrace new beginnings. Instead of focusing on the past, shift your focus to the present moment and the possibilities that lie ahead.

Here's how to let go of regrets and embrace new beginnings:

Practice Self-Compassion: Be gentle with yourself as you navigate feelings of regret and disappointment. Remember that it's normal to feel a range of emotions after a breakup, and it's okay to permit yourself to heal at your own pace.

Release the Need for Closure: Accept that closure may not always come in the form of a tidy resolution or explanation. Sometimes, closure comes from within, as you release the need for answers and find peace in the present moment.

Focus on What You Can Control: Redirect your energy towards aspects of your life that you can control, such as your thoughts, actions, and attitudes. Cultivate a sense of empowerment by taking proactive steps towards creating the life you desire.

Creating a Vision for the Future and Moving Forward with Hope

Despite the pain of a breakup, the future holds endless possibilities for growth, fulfillment, and happiness. By creating a vision for the future and moving forward with hope, you can reclaim your sense of agency and purpose.

Consider the following:

Set Intentions: Clarify your values, goals, and aspirations for the future. What steps can you take to align your actions with your vision?

Visualize Success: Use visualization techniques to imagine yourself thriving and succeeding in various areas of your life. Visualizing your desired outcomes can help manifest them into reality and inspire you to take action toward achieving your goals.

Stay Open to Opportunities: Remain open-minded and receptive to the opportunities and possibilities that come your way. Life is full of unexpected twists and turns, and by staying flexible and adaptable, you can seize the opportunities that align with your vision for the future.

Finally, honoring the past and embracing the future are essential aspects of the healing journey after a breakup. By reflecting on the positive memories of the past relationship, letting go of regrets, and creating a vision for the future filled with hope and possibility, you can navigate the challenges of heartache with grace and resilience. Remember, the end of one chapter is just the beginning of the next, and by embracing the journey of self-discovery and growth, you can create a future filled with love, joy, and fulfillment.

CONCLUSION: EMBRACING HEALING AND GROWTH

As we conclude our exploration of overcoming breakup grief, it's essential to take a moment to reflect on the journey we've embarked upon, celebrate the progress made, and embrace the possibilities for healing that lie ahead.

Reflecting on the Journey of Overcoming Breakup Grief

Throughout this book, we've delved into the intricacies of navigating breakup grief, from the initial shock and heartache to the gradual process of healing and renewal. We've examined the myriad emotions that accompany the end of a relationship, including sadness, anger, and acceptance, and explored strategies for coping and finding solace during pain.

In reflecting on your journey of overcoming breakup grief, consider the challenges you've faced and the milestones you've achieved. Recognize the moments of courage and resilience that have carried you through the darkest days, and honor the strength it takes to confront your emotions with honesty and vulnerability.

Celebrating Progress and Resilience

As you look back on your journey, take a moment to celebrate the progress you've made and the resilience you've demonstrated. Whether it's finding moments of joy amidst the sorrow, reaching out for support when needed, or simply allowing yourself to feel and process your emotions, every step forward is a testament to your strength and determination.

Acknowledge the growth you've experienced along the way, no matter how small or incremental it may seem. Celebrate the moments of insight, self-discovery, and personal empowerment that have emerged from the depths of heartache. You've demonstrated incredible resilience in the face of adversity, and that in itself is cause for celebration.

Encouragement for Embracing Healing, Growth, and New Possibilities

As you prepare to move forward from this experience, I offer you words of encouragement to embrace healing, growth, and new possibilities with an open heart and mind. Allow yourself to be curious about the future and the endless opportunities it holds for love, joy, and fulfillment.

Embrace the journey of self-discovery and personal growth that lies ahead, knowing that each step forward brings you closer to a place of wholeness and authenticity. Trust in your ability to navigate the challenges that may arise, drawing strength from the resilience you've cultivated along the way.

Remember that healing is not a destination but a continuous journey, and it's okay to take your time and honor your unique path. Be gentle with yourself as you navigate the ups and downs of the healing process, and know that you are worthy of love, happiness, and fulfillment in all areas of your life.

In closing, I want to express my deepest gratitude for allowing me to accompany you on this journey of healing and growth. May you continue to walk this path with courage, compassion, and grace, knowing that you are never alone. Embrace the healing and growth that awaits you, and may your heart be filled with hope, resilience, and boundless possibilities.

With warmest wishes for your continued journey.